An Orangutan's Story

BHAGAVAN "DOC" ANTLE

WITH JOSHUA M. GREENE

Photographs by the staff and friends of the Myrtle Beach Safari

INSIGHT KIDS

San Rafael, California

My name is Bhagavan Antle. You can call me Doc. I run a wildlife preserve called the Myrtle Beach Safari. Let me tell you about one amazing animal who lives with me at the preserve.

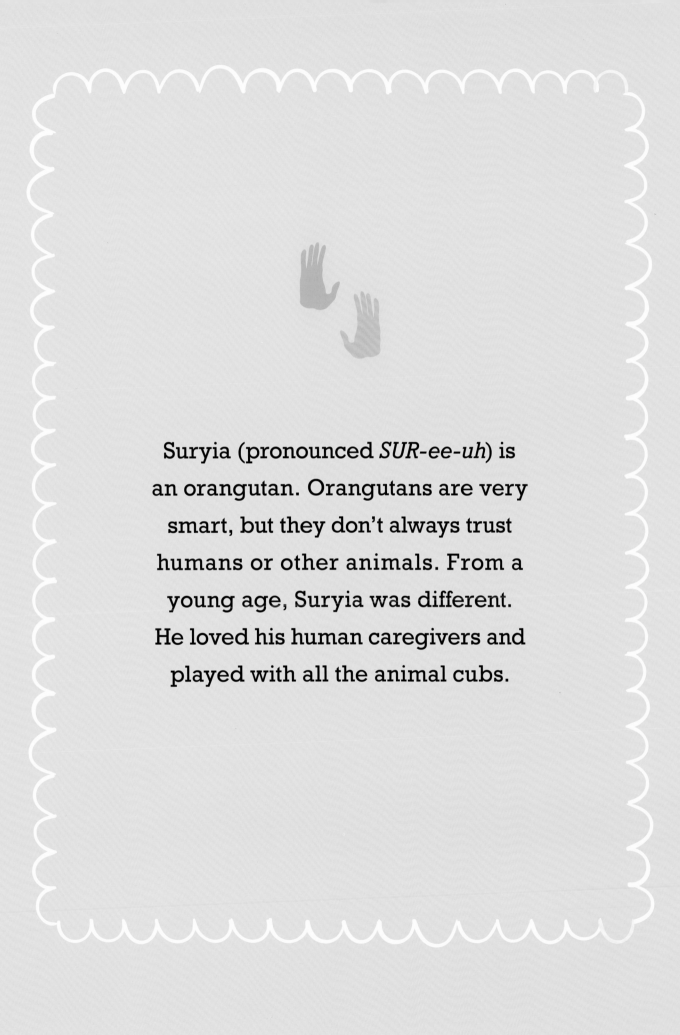

Suryia (pronounced *SUR-ee-uh*) is an orangutan. Orangutans are very smart, but they don't always trust humans or other animals. From a young age, Suryia was different. He loved his human caregivers and played with all the animal cubs.

When he was little, Suryia lived with his
family. He was the most curious of
all his sisters and brothers—and the most
daring. When Suryia saw Bubbles
the elephant out for a walk one day, he
jumped on her back. Riding
Bubbles became his favorite sport.

One morning, Suryia was riding
Bubbles around the preserve. Suddenly,
a scruffy hound dog stumbled out of
the woods. Bubbles the elephant stopped
to check out the strange dog.

As soon as Suryia saw the dog,
he jumped off Bubbles, ran over, and
hugged the dog. The dog put his
paws on Suryia's shoulders and licked
his face. This was very unusual.
Dogs are usually scared of monkeys
and apes. But this dog and Suryia
liked each other right away.

The dog had a tag with a phone number
on it. We called and found out the
dog's owner had moved away. Everyone
agreed that the dog should stay.
We named him Roscoe.

Each day, Suryia and Roscoe spent
hours running around the preserve playing
tag, hide-and-seek, and Frisbee, and
sometimes just hanging out by the pond.
Suryia went on walks with his dog BFF
and offered him monkey food. Roscoe liked
the biscuits, but not the bananas.

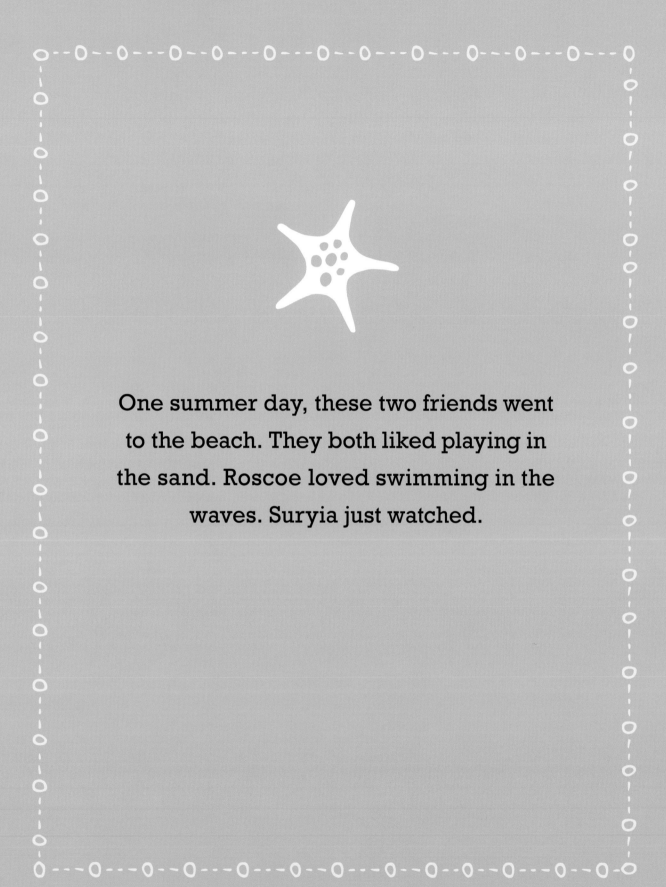

One summer day, these two friends went to the beach. They both liked playing in the sand. Roscoe loved swimming in the waves. Suryia just watched.

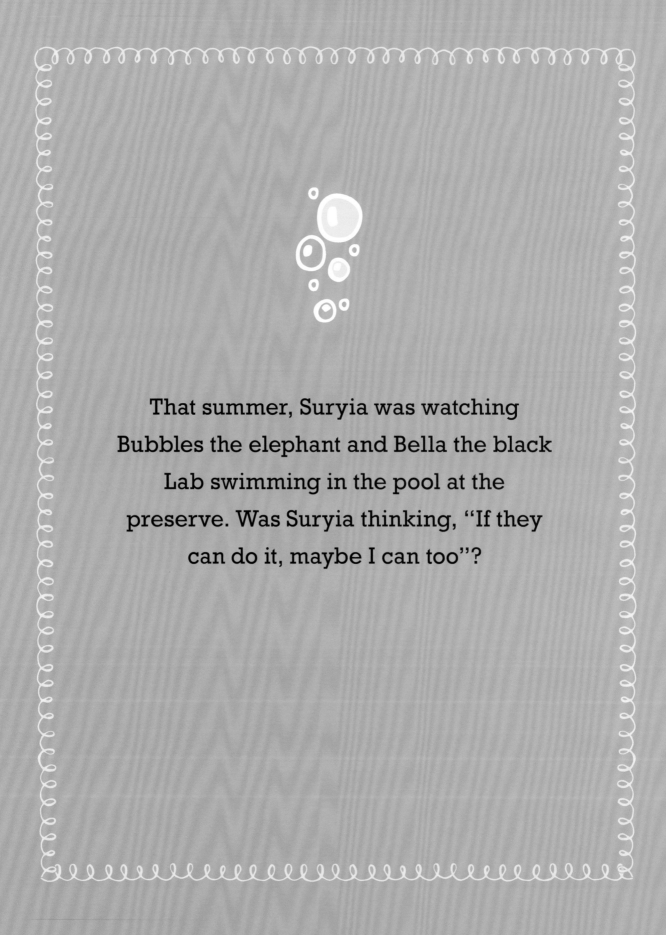

That summer, Suryia was watching
Bubbles the elephant and Bella the black
Lab swimming in the pool at the
preserve. Was Suryia thinking, "If they
can do it, maybe I can too"?

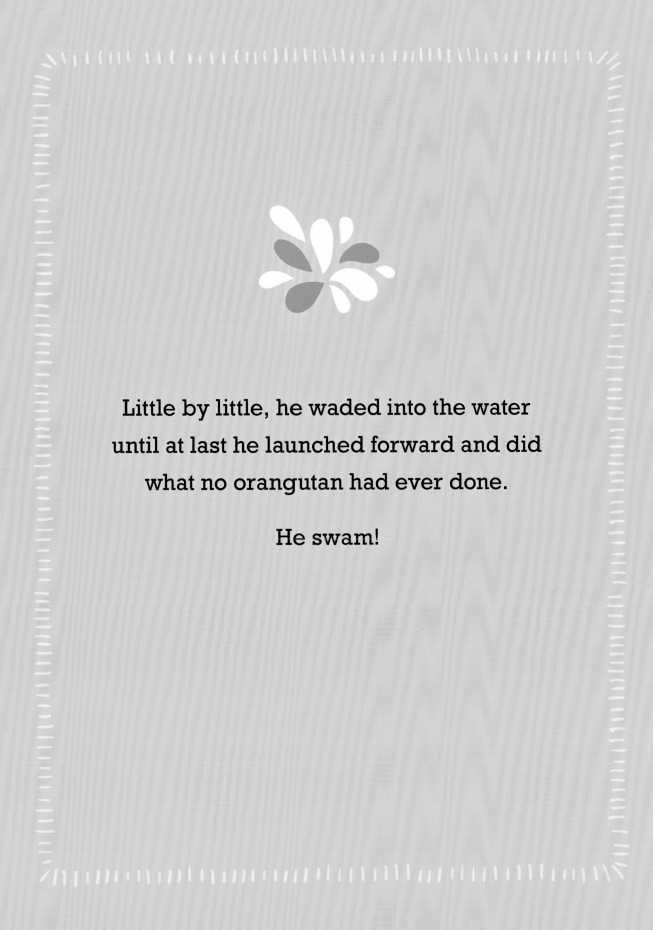

Little by little, he waded into the water
until at last he launched forward and did
what no orangutan had ever done.

He swam!

One of the people working at the preserve took a video of Suryia swimming and posted it online. In only a few weeks, Suryia became one of the most famous animals in the world.

People came to the preserve asking to meet the famous orangutan. Suryia was good at showing visitors around his home. They loved watching Suryia swim and take care of the baby animals.

Suryia's day ends around five o'clock
when he takes a bath and enjoys
one last treat—usually a peach. Then he
brushes his teeth and gets in bed.

Suryia is older now. He and Roscoe don't
run around the preserve as much as they
used to. Suryia and his friends like to stroll
together instead, smelling the flowering
trees, waving at animals, and watching the
sun set over the river.

A NOTE FROM THE AUTHOR ABOUT ENDANGERED ANIMALS

Orangutans like Suryia used to live all over Asia. But now there are only a few thousand left. We say that orangutans are *endangered*, and without help, wild orangutans may soon be gone.

Other animals, like tigers, leopards, chimpanzees, and elephants, are also endangered.

The Myrtle Beach Safari, where Suryia lives, gives protection to endangered animals and raises money for wildlife programs around the world.

These are some of the endangered
animals that live with Suryia.

African elephant

Chimpanzee

Bengal tiger

Lynx

INSIGHT
KIDS

An Imprint of Insight Editions
PO Box 3088
San Rafael, CA 94912
www.insighteditions.com

Find us on Facebook: www.facebook.com/InsightEditions
Follow us on Twitter: @insighteditions

Library of Congress Cataloging-in-Publication Data available.

ISBN: 978-1-68383-195-2

Publisher: Raoul Goff
Associate Publisher: Jon Goodspeed
Art Director: Chrissy Kwasnik
Designer: Evelyn Furuta
Editor: Molly T. Jackel
Project Manager: Joshua M. Greene
Managing Editor: Alan Kaplan
Editorial Assistant: Tessa Murphy
Production Editor: Lauren LePera
Associate Production Manager: Sam Taylor

ROOTS of PEACE   REPLANTED PAPER

Insight Editions, in association with Roots of Peace, will plant two trees for each tree used in the manufacturing of this book. Roots of Peace is an internationally renowned humanitarian organization dedicated to eradicating land mines worldwide and converting war-torn lands into productive farms and wildlife habitats. Roots of Peace will plant two million fruit and nut trees in Afghanistan and provide farmers there with the skills and support necessary for sustainable land use.

Manufactured in China by Insight Editions

10 9 8 7 6 5 4 3 2 1